KARMIC DEBRIS

The Poetic Writings of Piya Italia and Franke Wednesday

By Valerie and Peter Genovese

Forgotten Voices
From the 1960s & 70s

While every precaution has been taken in the preparation of this book, the publisher assumes no responsibility for errors or omissions, or for damages resulting from the use of the information contained herein.

KARMIC DEBRIS: THE POETIC WRITINGS OF FRANKE WEDNESDAY AND PIYA ITALIA

First edition. July 16, 2022.

ISBN: 979-8201729509

Written by Peter Genovese.

Table of Contents

This book is dedicated to the many pilgrims who shared the journey or the path with Franke and Piya... through the years: some of whom have fallen along the wayside, some... who have disappeared, and others, still strive on...

None have been forgotten.

A special thanks to Gianni C. for the Cover Design.

Marshfield Madness
(A deepening dependence)
Section One

It was autumn... 1970

Piya and Franke were driving towards the Massachusetts coast, speeding south away from Quebec City... their 1963 Rambler flashed past small French-Canadian villages. They had a wad of cash, no constraints, and no plans, except... being together.

They finally came to rest... at a lonely blue house, on the edge of a salt marsh,
with the ocean a short distance away, and the constant sound of the waves filling their subconscious. It was getting cold; the seasons were turning. Their big red dog lay outside, guarding the door, his face into the wind... waiting for the eminent winter to arrive.
And they heated the house with driftwood... blazing in the fireplace... with Piya's whispers in the night. The two of them... inside, safe, secluded... in love.

It was there they melded together; there that a mystical dialogue began between them, both simultaneously being... and resisting. There, that their fates were forever sealed.
Two sweet souls, gathering wood... on a windy beach
Two tiny specks, wandering, free... in the omnipresent emptiness.

Franke Wednesday (excerpt from The Narrow Path of Love)

Let's sleep, then drive

And lose all track of everyday time. What is offered?
Catch all we can.
As the dawn of silver and grey shadows awakens, the first snowfall.
Let's sleep then drive... and lose track of time,
in the dawn of the silver blue shadows

Piya Italia

Where do poets go...

If not back to their words,
not to someone else's hidden meaning.
What of the self is not your own?
How to express your quest? Mouth vexed... vital?
Questions tetter on the edge of an awesome decravity.

To live by the words, to stand by them...
Who will pay for that?
To be the exact measure...not a mirror held up
when certain broad categories are represented.
How to be viable... but still be allowed the title... Poet.
One conscious iota makes you a liar.
The uncertainties don't subside
They are like an infinite line of Persians popping up
on every rock at Marathon... nagging and intrusive.

There have been circular days and nights,
when the pressure of questions stabbed at sanity.
Yet, somehow, beneath it... hovering above,
lay an even more intense desire for the truth.
What is a poet's life but purgatory?
Franke Wednesday/ Marshfield, Massachusetts 1971

The Dream

The dream of rebelling against what I love came back early this morning. The single question of what to do with the emptiness that I have?

I can no longer fill myself with useless imaginary emotions. Disappointment comes and with it a reaction that indicates I am living a hollowed existence. There is something I should create – a single destiny. Satisfaction is only temporary. Why?

The negative force that makes me obstinate and uncontrollable could be the counter-self.

Accept nothing... aceptar nada.

Piya Italia

(*Used in the Aleph Null performance "In repression of preconception" 1973)

From the Window

What a fine day it is.
The clouds of murky white
block out the sunlight.
The river... running through the marsh, is dark blue,
high and choppy, heavy with the last of the mud, pushing through
... carrying a portent of the cold yet to come.
Stunted pines and March plants, choreographed by the wind,
dance... bending over the shoreline

Big boy lays on the ground,
his hair thick and blown
winter bound...
along the North Atlantic coast.
His greying face and clouded eyes...
scan 180 degrees... from shore
back to the front door...
watching, waiting for us.

Fall enters on cue,
the vanguard
of a summer here
we will never see.
Franke Wednesday/ Marshfield Mass. March 27, 1971

Toward the Sea

As you stare out the window... toward the sea there's a melody of questions haunting me. No pleading look or lonely sigh can force your eyes to mine.
Will I one day see you smiling
with a happiness of forgotten me?

Disappear... only words ring clear

Piya Italia
October 1969

A Wall of Answers

Hang your own picture on the wall of answers
keeping life in an order that reminds, resembles the future negative.

How to continue with the question of nothing.
Dream fantasies and the secret veil vibrated my very body into submission. All thoughts are given to the repair of self. Bandage around the brain.
I do wonder yet?... The reflection can lie.

Piya Italia

Highways in the Sky

Highways in the Sky, keep calling
don't go away... stay! I need you now more than ever
Let your breezes pull me float me away, on lanes away from today.

High in your lofty passes... naked against their perils. Permit me... to
challenge and be judged.
Cold and alone... spirit atoned

Open wide unknown lands, , free savage... horses let them race, heads
loose, backs bare...
across mystery haunted plains mile after mile.

Highways in the Sky! Your caravans drift from sight...
Are your strangers needful? Are your taverns full for the night?

Franke Wednesday/ Marshfield, Mass.,1970
Lyrics

The Right to Know

I'm seized by the right to know
and it doesn't hesitate to tumble in without warning.
My own desires and outside causes try to avoid it,
but it's to no avail.

Snowing in the window...
a chilly air sweeps the room
as the beauty of a memory surges above it.
Christmas mornings come to mind... and the pure, good feeling of
being alive.

Franke Wednesday/ Rochester, NY Fall 1969.

Christmas Trance

The Christmas trance has been full of worries.
What to give my mother? What reality am I now in?
Living in one place with quiet and snow or living in another, brown,
with nowhere to go?

Twilight hours then I can write.
A sleigh jingles by, then quickly leaves my burning sight.

Piya Italia December 19, 1971

The Pool of Waiting Souls

Your life is exhausted in unfailing anticipation of its prospective destinies.

So oblivious and nonexistent to you, that your future rushes in like a wave to become your present – and the water of flowing life is too powerful for you.

Nothing changes in your eyes, dreams of premonitions arrive, and you have the dazed look of mad knowledge that soon you will begin living... while the whole time it is passing.

All you have now is the "no-expectancy" pool of waiting souls like yourself.

Piya Italia/ September 16, 1970

In Dreams: A Circle of Dissimulation/ A Denial of Resignation

Her waking is like this:
("Piango quando sono malata")
"I cry when I'm sick"
("Mi irrigiodisco quando ammuffite")
"I tense when proven images become stale"
("Dalla fantasi di chi escono gli angeli")
"Whose imagination did the angels come from?"
("T santi, si arrendono a niente?)
"Do saints submit to nothing?"

His waking
Tender are the moments without her... about her,
while seeking a limitless boundary, desperately as a stranger
A life of knowledge... of unraveling essences,
affirming actions,
and unwavering, unswerving purpose
... with intent.
Even at the height of desperation, to happily cry
"In dreams, I slumber and slip away,
the dark tableau below,
with no concern for anyone... I await
dimensional slips, inner implosions,
the dream, dreaming free and unbounded, dreaming while awake
Free Mexico!

Her waking is much like this:
I wake often with repeating thoughts that I went to sleep with.
It is odd not to have something knawing within.

I feel silence... routines have blotted out reflections.
The cruel innocence of waking!
... I chose to sleep... longing for my dreams
"The distance is greater."
("La distannia e piu grande")
"The silence is deeper..."
("il silenzio e piu profondo")
"The void kinder"
("il vuoto e piu gentile")
Cowritten Piya Italia *and Franke Wednesday.* Child Street, Rochester NY

Dream Image

I fell asleep early morning
And shared a life not
like the most conscious one.
I felt a safety... almost immortal.

Piya Italia *September 26, 1972*

Searching for Truth

I notice a second dimensional life. But to capture control of the truth, I must secure possession of the secret.

It affects history and the future. The only reminders of a clue... come in calm dreams

Piya Italia/ *April 1972*

The Agonies of Love

Dark blue passion of tightly wrapped thighs
and atomic explosions of the dying size.
Hot blood runs through her mind and for a few seconds, she's a gypsy
bride...
screaming with the agonies of love

Piya Italia/ February 1970

Those deep breaths, Susie?

Franke Wednesday/ Warwick, RI 1971

"Oh, it can't be that bad!"
Let me explain...
Man erodes.
Destiny... is it worthy of devotion?
I see a rolling set of momentum... rushing across the galaxy... to what?
A striving for perfection a showering of uniqueness until the final
explosion ends it all.
What then?

Man erodes .... Through microcosmic expansions and withdrawals,
whether overwhelmed... or surviving
it inches along.
Various illusions infect the globe. They cross the oceans... enclosing the
land, filling empty spaces in minds with corrupt, magical incantations,
and hidden attempts at control... while all the time projecting
an Audie Murphy farce of heroics and absolute values.

I know, in the end... it is crucial to believe in something! To honor...
some form of rationality... to accept a truth worthy of devotion.
And yet... it all seems a manifest illusion
So, it's like that Susie.
I take a deep breath, let it out, and for the moment, I can carry on.

Tempting are the Patterns that Plague

It was morning. I didn't want to move from under the covers
to leave the nest... go out onto the barriers.
Life is a torrid mess... with tight tuned strings
astride foolish desires
and little future surety.

Not evolved enough for nirvana...
instead, I live on,
while happiness could... if only
the future waits,
the past wasn't quite
and the present seldom is.

Adrift amidst the wash of humanity... tossed
on the endless beach of our world,
seeking...making...failing...hoping...disappearing.
How kind to remember those from the past.
To give them momentary reflection,
amidst the existing reality.

Bobo cries. Is thrilled by devices.
She learns... as we watch the beauty of her beginning...
The world may erase her pure clean
smiles ... and her passing will... someday.
The awesome path of life confronts
the wheel of change.
Buddha Shiva Jesus
The great ones of the past,
was it all mystique?

Time possesses... and neither words, nor thoughts are eternal
But... is something... after death
unmortal
immortal?
super mortal
Franke Wednesday

Fragments

There are still only fragments.
So much of living is fragments.
Nulls' truth surfaces,
with anxieties over facts that confront and startle.
To be unprepared for it.
And if it ceases to be
and isn't anything more than cosmic vapors...
then all of this has been a neurotic waste.

Piya Italia

Memories

Memories enclose the crystal ball of my eye as I slip from the wall
and fall upon the breakers
only to reach for a good hand to guide me.

Piya Italia *September 23, 1968*

In Rebuttal

They had lived alone for some time: months, years... he couldn't say. No one had assisted them, nothing had injured them. Isolated as they were, tensions in Cairo or festivities in New Orleans never mattered. Heralding news came on the wind, keeping them informed on the fate of reeds, or the birth of creatures in the forest, the changing of seasons. Arguments over procedure never mattered... there was but one way, and he lived within it... yet unaware of it.

He never had to make decisions about speaking truthfully to others, nor needed to watch as real emotions were masked by disguises. He was a cell of nature; there were no divisions. Life guided him far better than outside influence and laws. There was the daily truth all around him, no need to question it. Time had ceased to be a carriage confining him, pulled by a human-led horse. He had escaped that prison, even as the ever-turning wheels of the carriage spun a message over and over: NEVER ALLOWED TO RETURN... Never Allowed to Return... never allowed to return

The message did not affect him. Above... the continuous sound of an airplane, circling, caught his attention. Electronic speakers blared above him, "We are here to help you... show yourselves!" There was no need for help. He felt her touch, a gentle brush inside his head. It said ... "Time to move on." The speakers blared, as the One of them vanished... melting into the forest... never looking back.

Franke Wednesday/ 1/15/ 1969... Rome, NY

Burning Streets

We were happy enough to be excited. A train was waiting to take us to Guatemala,
the Mexican Gulf breeze cooling us,
cash in our pockets.
A perfect day in Vera Cruz .... Steamy!

"What's that up ahead?"
An old Mexican man lying prone on the sidewalk... his pants partly down.
Dead drunk.... "Is he moving?" Sort of stiff.... face down pasty blood....
Hurt? Or dead?

The hot sun burned the pavement where he lay. People walked by... looking away. Life and the chancy extent of it trudged rudely and uncomfortably by.
Human loss, and the tenacity of life's grip seemed somehow weaker here in Mexico. The dangers of living less predictable less under control.

We walked past the man... Piya sobbed quietly with the thought of death and its implications so near.
Brutal and sudden existence... cloudlike wafted through us, and then, floated back into the ether.
We walked toward the train station, drawn to a straight rail for awhile

Franke Wednesday/ Vera Cruz 1971.

Tentative

The depth comes at moments that supersede all else.
I see facts I otherwise choose to avoid.
Death and everyday motions.
How to exist amidst those inevitabilities.
To bear the thought of endings and tragedy.
I have seen death slip into a living being's eyes
and in a fraction, an iota, nothingness existed
where once understanding and life issued.
What are we?
What can this mystery of existence be?

Shall I travel my time and share what beauty I can,
only to slip away in my sleep.
Will I never share the presence of my love?
... in another state?
Or is she only the darling of this life?

Franke Wednesday/ Cholula, Mexico
October 15, 1972

Secrets

Words secretly allow for the wonderment of
just exactly how it is. Oh, to be in sync.
On this evening – a saturated dew point gives a sullen, sultry veil. The
lethargic reasoning won't hold up much longer

Piya Italia

Wandering Soul

Wandering soul
always losing time
Wandering Soul
can't make up your mind
Never know which way to go
All you ever do is lose

Wandering Soul, test the time when right
change your phrase if wrong
never let down your guard.

It's a hard road
Out of sweat and into darkness
with confusion the reward.
The net goes... but one way
and you must enter without a knife,

Wandering Soul
Always losing time
Wandering Soul
Can't make up your mind
Never know which way to go
All you ever do is lose
Wandering Soul
Lyrics: Cowritten: Franke Wednesday & Piya Italia

Testing Fear

Testing fear will last past tomorrow, but don't walk on the warped boards, because there are miles of death under them.
Safety is clutched with sanity's noose gripped tightly around the neck.

Remember... if you writhe too hard, it is you who is the odd vision of pain

Co-written: Piya Italia/ *Franke Wednesday*

I am macaroni and bean soup

I am macaroni and bean soup
cauliflower and batter fried
tortilla rolled with meat

I am painting on a cave wall
sun worship and superstition...
cringing in fear of eclipse.
I am prayer

I grovel on the side of a cliff
bitter because of the cold
helpless against all

Savage and hungry
simple and lean
tense and afraid
I am nothing next to infinity

Franke Wednesday/ Rochester, NY 1973

Water Meter Reader

Canadian Geese fly high above, coming home in formation over the still cold lake,
a mere outline against the milky, cold clouds.
The world is grey except for their dark shapes.
Their flying lines, a borderland between earth and sky.

It moved him so this year, hearing their calls...
"Look, the geese are coming home!" he cried out pointing.
Walking alone on the cold, city streets...
in and out of basements, black and dank, reading meters,
the growls of dogs in the apartments above,
the furnace blowers kicking on.
Calling out... "It's the Meter Reader Man!"
Then... back outside, down different steps, into other cellars.

Yet... high up in the sky...
above the chill and greyness, are the lines of geese coming home,
instinct guiding them,
instinct guiding him.
A tear for the beauty of the geese
A tear for him...
Franke Wednesday

Mother

Today, especially, I feel so like my mother. It is I who prepares dinner on this foggy mountain.
My self... who remembers being in school and trying to imagine home... and my mother.
It is me who cocoons.

Piya Italia/ *Clinch Mountain, Va. 29 October 1980*

Hope

Time and again it rises...
hope... balanced, on brittle glass lances
supporting the monumental weight of future serenity.
Higher and higher... hope rises
then suddenly, it falls... shattering to the ground.
The bitter simplicity is immediately apparent.
Standing amidst the broken remnants of lost expectation...
disappointed... more hardened and cynical.

Who could have predicted the extent by which, the search... would test
and torment?

Franke Wednesday

Everyone's becoming powder

Love the rule
is disintegrating
Music is
disappearing
Friends are
failing at needs
Ten-year reunions
reuniting what?
I sit up late,
away from the crowd
When will the courage come?
Am I to find out that I did know
what I was doing?
These questions wait for answers.

But from out of the decades
a wisp of a challenge emerges...
Give up everything and search for aliens!

Franke Wednesday

Saturday Morning... 1977

Franke Wednesday

Care of Bolivia – the Bobo – Miss Aura, my child
A duty, a pleasure... an honor
Existing on four hours sleep
Working within the dichotomy...
Music... the persistent
Camera... the daily
Pen... the repressed

Marketing with father, brother, and child.
Hawkers, live ducks, dead fish ... mountains of produce
the world must eat; the world must sleep...
ritual exercises
Visit mother – coffee, coffee
Reconciling dreams to life activity
Traveling to the lake to share a meal
The world must eat; the world should laugh
Lawrence Welk... Pizza
Our child sleeps in peaceful slumber
Capsulize and plan... augur the future
... moments of passion

Shadows stretch across the drafting table
from one single light.
Outside... the darkness of night... the end of day
Bodies in bed... years before, years after, side by side
Man, woman, and child.

Lusty Images

She thinks metal boxes will hold her secrets,
but they only provide her
with lusty images she never knew
Her stomach is smooth to the touch of ice fingers.
Evil men are lucky they never knew her.

Piya Italia

Waiting

Your sight was failing, your body numb. We both waited until I could come. Block after Block, running against time
I felt the ache of your heart and mine you were hanging by a thread from death.
I pleaded and cried to feel I was there.
You whispered a word I never heard ... and the light left your eyes.

Piya Italia/ From a nightmare October 26, 1971

Who is closer?

Who is closer,
than one who has wrapped legs for warmth
or licked fevered eyes?
Who is closer,
than one who has linked
body to body in hard connection
slept side by side
starved when I starved
fought for me or died?
Who is closer?

Franke Wednesday

Shaking Earth

The slender ships have already met the stars in my mind.
Their nighttime sparkles... are constant and near.
Man's losses have paid the fare.
We have sent forth first... soldier explorers,
with cold masks of brave expressions.
Sent them further than they ever imagined.
With them, they bring back
a deepness always lacking.
They have wandered through God's mind
and returned.
Led by the first team
Everyman has peopled the stars, found, and lost worlds,
charted green moons.
In their new homes, they dream of
other mountains, recall dying seas.
They survive, breed, and forget.
Sent out, explored, and settled
encountered, been encountered – they continue.
In Ship worlds, armed and arm with life in its immensity
their squashed egos are proportioned by extraterrestrial realities.
Physical infinity stretches... in an unending frontier ahead.
Worlds of death and decadence
tests of endurance and adaptability
never imagined natural barriers.
Civilizations long dead discovered on countless worlds
threats to human existence... unending possibilities!

THUNDER!
Trapped on an outworld

where there is nothing else
and the stars are only dreams.
What to be, where to go...?
Let the sky open above me
Let me journey to where there is a choice!
New sights... new sounds... a limitless horizon.
Franke Wednesday/ Marshfield, Mass. March 20, 1971

Change

Caught in the middle of change
with growth and separation vying for attention. People all around all
demanding attention.
Little peace, no rest
only action (redundant action)
And thoughts, many different – thoughts—unconnected on separate
paths at the same time.
Decisions! Decisions crowd the day silence .... seldom found
aloneness... almost never
pace – blinding, confusing pace.

And at the same time...
Caught in the middle of change.
Shedding another skin .... blinding light! Stepping from the cocoon
into a whirling, birth morning.
Let a Mexican night of stillness drip serenity
on smoothly changing,
perfectly fitted gears.
I need an ancient tunnel, dark and musty.

Franke Wednesday/ Rochester, NY
September 7, 1972

Bobo discovers the moon

Returning in the evening, we parked the car and
began carrying her into the house.
Suddenly, she turned and pointed
straight up at the crescent moon.

Discovery by my child.
My child... my discovery.
Innocence and purity... each moment
her understanding of the world grows.
A world that will bring both confusion and wonderment.
What of innocence will remain?

Bobo found a little basset hound dolly today
whom she loved immediately and is now inseparable from.
She kisses my ear lobe and hugs me laughing.
At nineteen months... I am hers completely.

Franke Wednesday/ Rochester, NY
June 1977

I'm lost... you don't care

What's all this talk of love...
when your face tells the tale.
Eternity is the way we've talked about
but I believe... where are you?

Alone in a human meadow
with rain upon your face
While my body grows above the clouds ...
reaching for the stars

What if I reach it alone? What then?
Will I wander without my true love?
Where will you be?
Taking another lost man and
sending him out alone... on a stormy sea?

Franke Wednesday/ Marshfield, Massachusetts
January 1971
Lyrics

Suspended

When the music moves you
you're floating on a hot afternoon sea
burned by the sun, cooled by the water
transforming the land into champagne on ice...
Breezy glare...
Squinting, nearly weightless
And the beauty melts you, makes you
weep in the back of your eyes,
deep in your throat.

Coltrane's other side... Alice
Climb the Atlas Mountains on desert rhythms
with phantom-like strength... undefinable.
Skim over the dried-out African seabed...
keeping the presence of others from you.
In Alice's eyes... one could see
she had known so many distant realities,
that to talk was a burden and a shock...

On a caravan, puckering beneath a white, dry sun
the desert stretching forever – to age-old Timbuktu.
Only the motion of the camel keeps you in touch.
A fly buoy... guiding you back from far... far away.
Franke Wednesday/ Rochester, NY. March 26, 1972

Twi-night

f
a
l
l
i
n
g

Begin at the end... not the beginning
Struggling through transitions
compromising with truth...
There's little joy in acceptance
only never-ending exceptions,
critics with suggestions

Stop the process
begin at the end.

Franke Wednesday

Concrete Tunnel, Open Sky

Faces in autos... the people of Cleveland pass by.
An endless parade, each face, a private place, amidst the dream of
America.
Slithering arteries stream towards fuming factories...
the once prevailing, vital focus of the city... the lake...
Now lies choked and dying... in disgrace
Concrete tunnels,
Open skies
Concrete tunnels
Open skies

Teleporting through the artificial, uncontrolled environment...
escaping by
Route 77 Steering straight ahead; leaving it all behind
as Alice rises from the speakers...
swaying with Pharoah and the men around her, so far from ghetto
sound...
As train cars race alongside, going the opposite way
a subtle fragrance of individual freedom ...fills the car.
Concrete tunnels,
Open skies
Concrete tunnels
Open skies

Is the best the world has to offer... good enough?
The struggle cannot cease... or abate.
Pushing south towards Cholula... to Mexico... and a new fate.
Passing streets of houses... squares and rectangles.
A fleeting memory of an American Flyer village dissolves ...

as our bubble speeds through the atmosphere, floating on harmonic
wind...

In the night, a beam from a sickle moon... set high above Kentucky,
falls to the earth... illuminating rolling fields below as
acres of tobacco flames, row on row, glow in the moonlight.
Concrete tunnels,
Open skies
Concrete tunnels
Open skies

Alabama... endless backroads ... meandering through a countryside lost
in time.
As darkness falls... a spiderweb metropolis is backlit by a single
porchlight
somewhere along the Elk River, with the electric hum of crickets...
floating through the open car windows, the cool evening... enchanting
us.
We race through the night... gliding on spinning rubber wheels...
heading south towards Cholula.
Concrete tunnel,
Open sky
Concrete tunnel
Open sky

September 1972 (Co-written Franke Wednesday - Robert Genovese)

The Drift

How far will we drift from our course so long ago set?
Is it strangers we've become?
Where's the passion?
What power has driven it underground?

It's the seriousness, my love...
the devout way that isn't always easy to capture.
I have something to say...
There are forces of life wrapped with such confusion, that little else matters.

Cowritten Piya Italia/ *Franke Wednesday*
Marshfield, Mass. 1972

Confusion

Confusion is stress.
Stress is wear.
wear is death.

Where is death?

Franke Wednesday

Eyes Open

I wish my thoughts were concentrated on problems that eventually turned to a positive stability... without the moods in my life that cause conflict to my Self.
I learn fear... producing clarity when confused. Opening my eyes.
Is my true Self a ghost?

Piya Italia

A Dripping Night of Mexican Serenity

There is the horror of late, late nights...
when from the ancient town the sounds jolt you
Screams... a pig being attacked by a pack of starving dogs chased down
and ripped apart

The smell of oil and fumes of dirt ... hopeless people the need for walls
with broken glass on top...
and all the time...
the terrible sound of too many dogs... in desperate combat
over an animal... in terrified pain
I keep praying for the silence to come.

Franke Wednesday/ Cholula, Puebla, Mexico. 1972

Man Ray is dead today

The painter artist...
"The Poet of the darkroom."
"Last of the Red-Hot Dadas"
An American in Paris
after 50 years...
he'll remain
still evolving

While I ride,
wandering crosstown in New York City
vacillating...between the Siddha Yoga Dham
and the Theosophical Lodge
Knowing that... in the middle
Lies Art/ the Man
Art/ the word.
As it did for him
his Art...
in the center,
shrouded, surrounded... by mystery.
Man Ray is dead today, but not forgotten.

It is a lonely cell that encompasses
a person's love for their inner visions.
Sad... and often unrewarding,
attempting to manifest those... private revelations,
converting an inside vision... to the outside,
stretching the boundaries of perception,
suggesting the irrational, the improbable...

Man Ray is dead today... in Paris
as the world goes on.
Franke Wednesday/ New York City November 18, 1976

Let Me Go

Artaud
Rimbaud
Cocteau
Let me go
I'll pray for you.
This week, save... eat your neighbor!
Buddha Beware
Fighting for the right of alternate dimensions
I seek to be truly a foreign element

Franke Wednesday/ Rochester, NY
1973

Lone Wolf

A wizen old man once told me
life taught that we could only do a few things
and everything else was taken up by the Gamekeepers.
He whispered...
"Secretly, running from hill to hill are a few mavericks – cheaters –
who travel their own way, follow their own path."
"They are hunted, discouraged, silenced by their exclusion.
But still... they run."

He said, "Be that.'
"Don't hide behind the rules,
Don't let the inside of the box cover tell you what to be,
or blind you from all other methods or pathways."
"If you must hate... hate the Gamekeepers... or the Keepers of the
Gamekeepers."

I said, "But if I run with these cheaters, I'll follow rules against the
Gamekeepers... still rules."
Just another group, outside the group, but still a group.
Isn't that a trap?"
The old man looked up at me...
his eyes red and almost myopic... and he said,
"Then become the Leader... the maker of rules.
Follow your own beliefs."
"And if not that... then be a Lone Wolf."

And I pondered... Leader or Lone Wolf?
Franke Wednesday

Children's Choir

The congregation, well suited, faced foreword
while we in the balcony, alone and unobserved,
set the mood for Reverend Hicks and Christmas.
Our sweet, young voices reverberated with songs of heritage and
innocence.
My turn came... and strange echoes spread through the rafters.
Hallowed sounds that rang.
It was during the second verse of Silent Night that a young man...
came closer to God... then ever before.

Franke Wednesday/ Rochester, NY

The Net

You've got to get together
for that big day
even if it means them
carting you away. The net goes but one way
And you must enter
without a knife.

Piya Italia

A Nagging Itch

It seems like there's nothing...
it always comes back to that.
No reason to go on...
but the simple fact of existence.

No place to run... no place to hide
But... suddenly, tonight... amidst the questions,
while living in thoughtless innocence...
a vision suddenly emerged.
Even the light – my senses – become more distinct.
It suggested that there is something that I've missed!
It's like a nagging itch whose exact spot can't be quite determined.

Then...it came to me... I'd found it!
Knock... Knock, Knock!
"Boss, wake up!!"
"What is it?
It's finally arrived!"
Franke Wednesday

When the blood is running free

That's when I'll finally be...
On a hot day... with all my senses
sweat cleaned.
I'll dance with the wind...
race the rain.

Time unraveled,
I can at last answer Wakan Tanka's call
and hunt the high, cool, green mountains,
where waters rush... fast and rock-flavored to the sea,
and the nights... are crisp and quiet.
With moonlight reflecting... and the evening stars shining above
I will lean my head back, as the sky wind blows my face and neck hair,
and I will howl for joy!

Franke Wednesday/ Marshfield, Massachusetts. April 16, 1971

Moments of Revolt

Not in front of me will I witness the sickening look of desperate need.
I close my eyes to the revulsion that surrounds me, as the noise gathers
with shrieking roars.
There is no place where I can go.
Anticipation meets its death in moments of revolt.

Piya Italia/ *December 31, 1971 Rupert, Vermont*

The Mundane/ the Sublime Truth

Living in the mundane world.
Understanding its balance.
Caught within its action; challenged... tempted by it.
Yet still longing for the sublime...wishing to reside in it.
Wanting my children to do more than just... sense it in me.
Needing to show them the way to reach it...
what is required to express it,
showing them that it's there,
and there is an evolutionary disposition towards it.

When I sense the sublime... inside... or on the outside of my children,
or they... sense it in me.
God... the Great Mystery is sending a powerful message
that we foolish humans, even amidst doubt and fear,
must embrace... far more fervently... sublime truth.

Franke Wednesday

Thin Facts

The facts feel thin to me.

I want to uncover a layer and see new depth inherit that deeper stratum
of existence... Fast!
To rid the body of toxic everything,
alone... in a pattern of solitude.

Piya Italia

Dark Ages

The setting: (A darkened stage... in the background... low feedback explosions are heard intermittently. A solitary figure with the wild hair of a prophet, stands under a single spotlight from above.)
The Prophet speaks to no one who listens. Behind him is a scene of a deteriorating cityscape

"Civilization is disintegrating, approaching the point of disaster and collapse.
The walls are coming down!
The beast is loosed again!"
"Run, flee for your life!"
"Seek the little used road, avoid the scenic by-way.
Find the solitary valley, where safety lies in lone-ness and all is prepared for survival."
"The fury that man's nerve center has contained... will attack and control the mob. It has it already."
(a chorus of voices speaks in unison...) "Unevolved instinct..." over and over...
The figure listens and then speaks again:

"Bleak limits will be placed on you. Your children, growing separate from you already, could be lost to its sordid influence. Constant fear will stifle growth!"
"You must run! Heed the warnings... they are everywhere!"
(The harshness of the spotlight fades and becomes a hazy blue)
The figure speaks softly now...
"We must get away. We must take ourselves and our lonely love to where it can still be enshrined and protected."
(Chorus chants) "Self-induced protection... free from detection!"

The Prophet becomes disturbed again... more desperate. The spotlight turns bright white again.

"Evolution will lose its most valuable adaption; the curtain will fall on city after city, country after country. Darkness will shadow continents."

"Violent death will stalk the earth with abandon... joined by its' cohort of Ignorance!"

"Delicate beauty will lie face down in the mud, raped and bayoneted, her child's body ripped and crumpled."

"Oh, the tears!... Weep for the dead!

This is not just a vision... save our genes of regard, originality, compassion, awareness!"

"Run! Speed away...

Guard your mind! Love your Self!"

"Darkness and blackness are waiting to put the whole known world under its sway."

"Pockets of life, the legendary Lys*, must be ready... a home for the future must be prepared and hidden."

"We will have to forget the stars. Our descendants will have to wait.

The Fools... the throwbacks are too many!"

"Disguise your brittle bones ... and disappear!

(Chorus) "Disappear, disappear... disappear..."

(The light slowly fades out... the figure sits, his face in his hands, weeping...

feedback explosions intensify... then fade out. The stage goes dark.)

Franke Wednesday/ Rochester, NY
December 21, 1971
*For Lys...See: The City and the Stars, (aka) Against the Fall of Night by Arthur C. Clarke

Clenched Thoughts

From within...
smelling the odor of vulgarity abandoning any desire to pursue such a
haunting thought.
White... while waiting with clenched thoughts.

So difficult to repeat the moment,
even for accuracy.
Triangles, chimes – drums and screams. I learn musical flow through
silence.
I feel invisible.

Piya Italia

On Watch at Light Speed

We had broken the barrier of the Sun. Stretching specks outside the ship testify to the
speed by which we roam. There's a terrible price to pay for such gluttony. The curse of a solitary world was not for me... with but one day and night. I fled to the desert city to find my place in the heavens, a solitary man.

Outward bound on a training mission, leaving behind age and its normal growth. Knowing that if or when we return, there will be no home, no family, no life once known. The passage of clock days did not stop us; light speeds slowed the scythe.

There is no place to rest or touch a relaxed nerve. Nothing that helps. We see only more and more of what was never known. The mind cannot rest on a familiar spot to put it all into perspective. Instead, there is never ending space, bringing with it another quest and another. Where are my mother's arms or my father's knowing eyes?
There!... in the lights of the viewport to cry to.

Franke Wednesday

In the Clinch

Music has filled an emptiness vacuum
When most other things have failed
It has kept my mind whirling,
droning with a concentration
that blocked out reality

Alone on a Colorado night –
wandering in a chill –
afraid to plan...
I have seen a stage and drums
beating for sanity's sake –
the sound a loud blur.
Eyes down
Arms flailing
Movement hovering on the edge of control
Transporting me away from rooms
filled with thick thinking people
I remember elevated times, without words,
only soaring melodic lines and flawless rhythmic changes,
and the swelling applause of the crowd

Time passes... memories fade, but this I know to be true...
if it is not the whole, music has always been a great fraction:
a sealing bond – a sacred blessing
It has saved my life when little else seemed to matter.
It holds... and will always have... a place in the master plan
It is a precious current running through everything
Franke Wednesday/ Marshfield, Massachusetts
March 25, 1971

A Cold Night in a Small Club, at the Bering Strait

Blank Faces stare back, as hours of attempt and dedication fall on deaf
ears.
Exploratory advances find solitary points of attention, isolated
in a wall of clanging glances and swollen glands.
We flash sardonic remarks, to low growls with unnatural requests,
as time drags by with short bursts of hope, hesitation... and moments
lost in song.

In between, time is filled with:
nothingness... bodily fear... libation
minor moments of glory... forgetfulness
and a sad awareness of the humanity in it all.
Another cold waiting room bends the ticking minutes,
as one swinging light, shadows...blinds...and shadows.
A hard seat to take is eased down on... vision is in black and white.

The years have worn away the thrill of being the topic of glances on first
entrance,
it is a fleeting pleasure. Belief in the image has long been replaced by
motivation
and striving for precision.
Over and again, it happens...
Then, weakened by heat and effort, we pack up our instruments of
presentation
and walk slowly out of the darkened hall, to another smoky room and
another sleeping bull.

Epilogue: Why?

At night it comes following numbing moments over the right word,
or the perfect syncopation, when the purpose seems obvious... and the
whole trail of pursuit is immediately visible.
It is in these spontaneous bursts of genius, in deep night's inhale that
keeps one going...
waiting for the next vision to manifest.

Franke Wednesday

The Drummer

I feel the native beat thanks to the drummer with his music like a lonesome train.
He's always dreaming of a song.
Only me, in my lost world, listens to this drummer. He never forgot my everlasting love.

An ache, a pain - alone

Piya Italia

Inevitability

There is I
and there is them
of which I am a part.
Within each,
there is a position of...
I and them.
When the question flares,
and it is deep,
the lack of the past becomes apparent,
but in this world, bearable, forgivable...
And there is cohesion, closeness, common purpose,
the love of music, future plans, reliance.

My I disputes the family,
even as the We... forms it.
There is not enough for a final split
or a union of consciousness,
as cycles of etheric drift occur.
In the end, the I will inevitably triumph.
All of us will go our separate ways... following different paths.

Yet... when the night fires dim,
and life becomes a red ember in a darkened room,
I will remember them all... with a sad loose love.
Franke Wednesday/ Rupert, Vermont. January 4, 1972

His Virgin Woman

I am his virgin woman
can you not tell?
My eyes could play with anyone
and sincerity is flowing.

My time is not now - an
early birth I have had - will
there be a long-time death?

I've tried to throw myself
out in time – lonely to do
alone. But for now
smiles are...for me,
the past burned black.

Piya Italia

Our First Home and We in Devotion

We'd lost our voice because of her
and our heart to her... as our first home
said good-bye, and we
bid her a most tearful adieu.
It was here in this place, that we learned our
most convincing lessons in devotion.
And seeing our ugly face momentarily
after the beautiful, left us ajar.

But, the house, our home... with its novel allure,
silently slipping back into oblivion slumber,
made sure we would remember... with one final gesture!
And we loved her more for that lesson.
Sleep sweet
Farewell...

Franke Wednesday/ Marshfield, Massachusetts
April 26, 1971

The Narrow Path of Love
Section Two

The Blue Condition

Miles has carried me through emotional delirium "tremors."
His music
has exceeded,
succeeded
in leading me
beyond disastrous distractions...
to a calm, safe harbor

Explain it away as... pure emotion
Or... that it speaks directly to the inner self.
Or perhaps it triggers a form of metabolic brain wave activity
of a perfected form.
In any event,
when Being
or trying to Be...
or perhaps... Being for the first time
little else suffices
... but Miles.

He comprehends...
absorbs the blue condition.
And I've never seen
so many hues
as on this catastrophic plummet...
through tragic love...
and its aftermath.

Even the bright red glare of the sun
so hard and so intense

Even that bright light... cannot not obscure it
The deep blue Is evident
in conversation
in moments alone,
when I sleep... or when I dream
It all comes back...
back to her and I.
No way to veil it
or to change it
No way to heal it
or forget it

The blue in green
The blue of the sea
The blue on the wall...
down the hall
The blue in the sky
The blue of her eyes...

The blue condition.

Lyrics. Franke Wednesday/ 11/22/02 The Studio, Tucson, Arizona

Your Light Touched Eyes

I've missed the day I'm living now. My yesterdays are hazy. Once he was opposite to my sensitive reactions. Nothing can happen overnight. Where is your reality? he asks.

I see it clearly.
You've made me feel the ruby red of warm caresses from your light touched eyes.

Piya Italia

Shed Suspicion

Shed Suspicion
as I shed deception...
Shed guarded words
as I shed... animal emotion
Strike viciousness and evil
thoughts from your mind.
Try to see each action I do
and just why I do it.

You tell me... it's an imposition
on a dream condition
that started long ago
but... it's just a state of mind
There are no contradictions in my heart
If I can rise above my faults
you can rise above your fear

You've got to... shed suspicion
as I shed deception
Shed guarded words
as I shed... animal emotion
Strike viciousness and evil
thoughts from your mind.
Try to see each action I do
And just why I do it.

You've got to feel it... feel it
I'll reel you in as fast as I can.
You've got to take it

You just can't fake it... anyhow
You can't run from it... love is changing all the time
If you don't hold on tight
it'll tear you up inside

You've got to,
shed suspicion
as I shed deception
Shed guarded words
As I shed... animal emotion
Strike viciousness and evil thoughts
from your mind.
Try to see each action I do
And just... why I do it.

I lay awake the night away...
lingering hopes still plan our day

Lyrics
Franke Wednesday/ Rochester, NY
1973

Piya's Moments

For me .... It's been a long and difficult immersion into a tangled reality;
quite complex.
Everywhere and nowhere Everything or nothing Remembering... who
I was seeing who I've become.

No sooner is there a brief ray of light and then the voices come
muddling up the view,
one thing after another.
And then... the slow dawning ... the shock of reality. Will you find it?
Can you? Is there time?

My moments drift by, bobbing in a deep, dark, troth... varied... and not
contiguous; it splits
up ahead, veering aimlessly from channel to channel... flowing through
dense, heavy subterranean sub-conscious. The troth wanders endlessly
through dark corridors... until! suddenly... caught in rapids, it rushes
through a narrow opening...
entering a cavern full of wonders... it cleaves into translucent crystals.
Hope the eternal returns.
Astonishments echo and reoccur.
Then... just as suddenly,
it is back into the troth.

***

Piya attracts the essence. She worries about everything, everything that
matters, everything that is not superficial, or assumed... not supposed,
or self-consumed.
She is the antithesis of the Search

In Piya's moments.... bliss slides on a silken thread following the sweet
simple connectors in life,
knowing that they are all that really matters, because within them...
everything is contained.

Franke Wednesday

The Wait

Anxieties obscured...
intuition slow.
The heart trampled
must endure the wait,
and a mystical patience maintained.
There is no other way.

Piya Italia

Cloud Limbo

Dance with me one last time, my love,
forget the cloud-limbo we live in
Close your eyes...
sway with me... glide to the music...
imagining I'm the man of your dreams

Our eternal bond is hanging by a thread
too easily broken by hopelessness and disappointment.
Spread your golden magic a final time.
Let me feel that assurity... with the proper lighting
softly... gently
without crashing lifetime monuments.
Are we to be merely statistics... living illusion,
lost people, too burdened with ancient selves
and planned expectation?

Let the days of hot clubs
and hurried meetings seep back in.
Remember the unknown houses and strange beds...
silk dresses and black suits pressed together.
Let me hold you in my arms once again, and believe...
believe it's the truth
that life is not a one-way... trans-Siberian highway.
Let our hearts flow together... be mine again.
Franke Wednesday

Living Jazz

I've painted my face to entertain you. No reason, except the world is
wide... and my smiles are not.

Adventure can't be dreamed of. I want more than old songs
that echo senseless words in my world.
Slipping, I get caught in my own throat and it feels like thick garbage.

Living right now reminds me of an old jazz record.

Piya Italia 2/5/71

Poems come

My mouth shapes the words,
but no breath follows.
I am worrying about myself.
By what existence am I living?
Tears and smoke supply the soul.
Nothing is external.

Piya Italia

A Revolution

Oh, what must I do to halt living in this pent up explosive frustration?
Forsake what I thought were my needs?
Exist without want? I am disjointed only by myself and a worn-out old master plan of life.

There is a revolution within ... humanism.
I'll go to Amsterdam.

Piya Italia

The Narrow Path of Love

Things were falling apart .... dissimulating
Franke felt it
on the outside, near the boundary line.
Vague signs of flaking, crumbling around the edges.
He was in a state of liminality, trapped on the borderland.

And he thought,
We move through life believing we've created
a system,
a pattern,
a tradition
until we reach a threshold of questions.
Then, within the inner self, thoughts begin to occur
And with the dominion of thought... actions
at first small... inconsequential,
slowly becoming dominant....
then overwhelming... obscuring everything,

Maybe it's doubt ....
Or age
Life... moving towards closure
The passing years
The accumulating bundles of time and experience....

How will it end for each of us?
What will we come to regret?
Where will the collateral damage be?
What will we wish we had done?

Things were unraveling... deep inside
Franke was concerned.
He had begun thinking about the past,
earlier times, people he had forgotten, places and purposes left behind.
People can be so foolish
we think we know what life is about
But few of us perceive life in its immensity
stretching into the universe... infinitely,
five dimensions in every atom
nothingness and diversity.

***

Everyday it's getting closer....
Franke could sense it.
Signs of things going slightly askew out there on the periphery.
Where would it end? What does it matter?

He knew no one ever really resolves the "if onlys"
if only he did this or if only... she did that.
We've all made our choices
whether to or whether not to?
Some are carried forward
others are left behind.

Franke choose Piya
Forsaking all the others...other paths... other people.
Though she wouldn't agree... she'd say,
"He never choose me."
And so, they lived within that duality
Hers: "Love is a trap if it changes at will"
His: "Love is a trap if it doesn't."

The road had been long and complicated for Piya and Franke,
and they'd traveled on a very narrow path.

Franke was remembering that hopeful autumn season.
He and Piya were driving towards the Massachusetts coast
coming south from Quebec City.
Their car flashed through the French-Canadian villages.
They had a wad of cash in Piya's purse, no constraints or plans
... except... being together.
They finally stopped at a lonely blue house set on the edge of a salt
march
with the ocean a short distance away, and the constant sound of waves
surrounding them.
They heated the house with driftwood that they collected on the beach.
Each evening the fireplace blazed...
warming them along with Piya's whispers in the night.
Their big red dog lay outside guarding the door during the day
his face pushed into the wind, waiting for the imminent winter to
arrive.
The two of them inside safe secluded
in love... a perfect circle,
Piya, Franke, and Big Boy

It was there they melded together
There that a mystical dialogue began
and a life of simultaneously being and resisting began
Where Franke's fate was sealed…
… so tight was Piya's lock around his heart.
These were the early steps on the narrow path

It was in Marshfield that a developing tension began,
and a vibration… that was so subliminal,
it was impossible to define
and so basic… it was unbearable to resolve
and so constant… it was improbable to believe
A dangerous and difficult reality
even when wrapped inside their own cocoon,
their own fiercely private envelope,
under the blanket of protection

that they called... Love.
God only knows what Love really is.

***

But it was slipping slowly away.
Franke knew it
so... he sought to pull himself together
back into the cocoon, back into the envelope, and then to seal it.
He began thinking about Piya and himself
remembering two sweet souls gathering wood on the windy beach,
back in the days of the lonely blue outpost.
Two tiny specs wandering and free
in the omnipresent emptiness together.
He and Piya.

***

And so it was, that Franke began again
Still, he wondered.
Where will the envelope journey to next?
Through another winter storm?
Or perhaps... into seclusion again,
where they'll watch the sea .... once more
the sea ... ever changing
pounding in on the coast
with the sound of the waves enclosing everything.

There, safe... deep inside their own cocoon.
with the path still winding a ways ahead
... a bit further to travel together.
And Franke thought....
Where will it take us next?

90

Where will the path lead?

What's next... on the Narrow Path of Love?

Audio script, Franke Wednesday

Paths to Infinity
Section Three
Piya Italia.

A quote: from Dana Burnet:
"Who dreams shall live! And if we do not dream, then we shall build no temple into time".
Unity Volume 79 #2 Cover, Congress of Religion, March 8, 1917. Who dreams shall live, Dana Burnet.

Introduction

The verse has always been sub to me – rarely shared
and protected like a diary, having had to maintain, and adapt often in
the past years...
I am able only recently to give my words the attention they deserve (or
so it has been told to me) allowing a very layered aspect of my Self to
emerge.

My domestic schedule gives me a very viable excuse... not to produce,
and to be emotionally unaffected as possible... it draws so much energy.

Sharing my thoughts and writings... remains counter to my instinct.

Piya Italia

Don't talk about it

... it fades.
Her paleness contrasted so
Passé yet vividly with her urgency.
She felt viewed, subjected and
was eventually numbed.

Liaisons, lawsuits, left-handed lover.

Piya Italia

Autumn remains late this year

A reminder to witness its assured departure. Through the coming year I will take strength from my memory of the fall. I need those scarlet nights when the world is white, so goodbye brown earth... to be complete with expression I must dance alone.

Piya Italia/ December 8, 1971, Pinnacle Hill

Living in Cycles

In the newness we parade
In the cycle worn bodies we adorn
Champagne for spring,
we shed a vapor
Mint Julep for summer,
we absorb
Wines for fall,
we intensify
Cognac for winter,
we adhere

Taut almost rigid I become
remembering the dualities

Hot – oh it is hot, and I'm hot
Silver shoes are hot
Silk suits are hot

Piya Italia

Thin Ice Under Heavy Words

What disease was caught when I grasped for a last hope? We used to roll in ecstasy together until you burst your guts. Since then, I've had to oppose you on many occasions... thin ice under heavy words

A blankness is draining,
questions give way to the definite words you sing

Piya Italia

The Human Parade

Sacrifice Calypso music in a red lace dress?
Fever from the sun exists in the moonlight. My intentions for unity of
my Self only brought loneliness.
Now, is death so sweet with its false coloring on my cheeks?
Shall I free my self-denials
and join the human parade of regrets?
Never!

Piya Italia

New Combinations

I prepare and dispose of instances that tarnish the established patterns. Often it is unavoidable, a repetitious syndrome that severs the emotional calm.
Oh echo... echo truths to me. Lead me away from this self-imposed paralysis

Piya Italia

Where?

Something is wrong when I feel the anxieties... a warning to understand my present existence.
Like the city pound searching for a full load of dogs, my ruthless mind is bewildered.

The final end?
Oh, where... where have I reasoned with a purity?

Piya Italia/ *August 9, 1971*

The Aftermath of Habit

Revolting the spiritual quest making most attainment fleeting
Passe'd plans that tend to inhibit if only from lack of actuality
Fewer photographs to aid the failing memory
Rejoice, shed the binding attachments! If only it were that easy

Piya Italia

Holy Minutes

She jumped on the wagon without any promises to God. And then she indulged with a renewed sense of discipline, cherishing the holy 47 minutes upon finding herself alone. (If only to make a late sauce for dinner)

Piya Italia

Colliding Thoughts

The penalty of having more than a single self is tormenting when opposite thoughts collide. Moments and moments disturb the guilt.

Try to return to the truth. How many variations are there? Falseness with a smile can create a sick impression. The kisses are too warm... I can't breathe.

Piya Italia

Reassessments

You finally arrived via my early morning dream
kissing my temple, exclaiming its softness and
proclaiming your love. They get misdirected
or become disaffected.

I knew I was dreaming – the state
of another illusion, but I was reluctant
to chase away such a simple
demonstration of happiness,
and I allowed my body to
sink lower in the
sub... and you continued to
press your lips to my temple.
Suffocation –
Fast love

Piya Italia

Paths to Infinity

When my Self denied me positive actions, I stopped.
Where was I?

The drawing of my paths to infinity covered the ugly confusion.
I screamed to be untouchable. Then a new tenseness grew, and I learned
to cry for an ache, a pain.

Piya Italia/ *April 28, 1972*

A Lost Light

There are certain things they never did only because they never thought of doing them.
If she had grown with ideas that halt imagination, she would be satisfied.

The positive and the negative collided with beautiful potential, but it slapped the essences around so they were permanently damaged – and the twinkle dimmed to a lost light in the sky

Piya Italia

This perfect clearness

This perfect clearness has to be constant. I watch how others attract their own kind, jellying together. Tension in my back reminds me that I scream for my own pain; there is no artistry in a liar.

Piya Italia

Her conscious thoughts brought anguish.

What remains should be precise
Forbid inward ignorance
Explode in secret if you must

Piya Italia.

The Annals of Later Times

Section Four

Franke Wednesday

The Gunas of 1998

In the Bhagavad Gita, it speaks of the three Gunas
states of mind, states of being, the way we function in life
Action – Raja
Delusion - Tamas
Wisdom - Sattva

Most of us are lost in raja continuous action filled with passion and confusion
with life, so complex at times, so difficult... so extraordinary.
We fill our lives with careers, with friends, we create activity, pay the rent, struggle with bills... conceive, deceive, reprieve, ... ephemera fills our days, loneliness, and passion our nights.
Sometimes we forget about everything but the minutia

Then, there is the sad and dangerous group of people, numbering in the millions, who are bound by delusion... called Tamas, cloaked in darkness and chaos. It entails danger, manipulation, misdeeds, and death.
Sometime... it feels as though the world is breeding people driven by tamas far faster than any other. Tamas infects the weak, consumes the misdirected and the indecisive.

There is a far smaller group... who live by wisdom seeking, goodness and harmony, compassion... those people live in the guna... Sattva.
They are found where need is the greatest: embracing the poor, the lost and the forgotten. Seldom are they observed in government... but when they are... they are beloved.

Billions of humans populate this world... buzzing and careening through life. Given the reality of raja, the overburden of tamas... it is amazing that there is any order at all.

Pray for a world clothed in sattva.

Franke Wednesday

Karmic Debris

We are all prisoners of our own mistakes,
mistakes we imagine we didn't make.
The fact is... that life is all about mistakes
striving for perfection... but failing much of the time,
with cherished moments in between.
It all becomes... Karmic Debris

Time
my time
times past
The ancient past...
shaping us
Our parents
molding us...
Our reactions...
changing us.
A chain of karmic disturbance
reaching back to the Rift Valley
... genetic trace material.
Karmic Debris
Karmic Debris

Inaction... leading to... over reaction
evolving, integrating.
We... influencing others
They... affecting us
as the ancestral necklace grows,
complicating, lengthening, intertwining.

Time

my time
times past...
illusions
delusion
sacred teachers
heroes
false prophets
failed assumptions
pushing this way
then, pliantly... pushing the other.
Perceiving
fictional misinformation... as truth
Misrepresenting fact...
to serve our own purposes...
As the karmic fragments remain

Time... going by
my time
your time
a finite rhyme
generation after generation
The past... to the future
reactions
accumulating
Karmic Debris

Indecision...
evolving,
negating,
integrating,
repeating...
the wheel ever turning

desperate exigencies
become karmic necessities

Time... passing
disappearing
running out
Striving... improving
our condition,
reconstituting
self- modifying
ever endeavoring
to refine...
to purify.
In the interim... decades pass
Time
our time
time left
Piya's time
your time
my time
Everyone facing time
slipping by
... diminishing
Trying to clarify
to rectify
identify
striving to
pacify
Time...
and Karmic Debris,
Karmic Debris
Franke Wednesday

The Four Rooms... "Wake Up!"

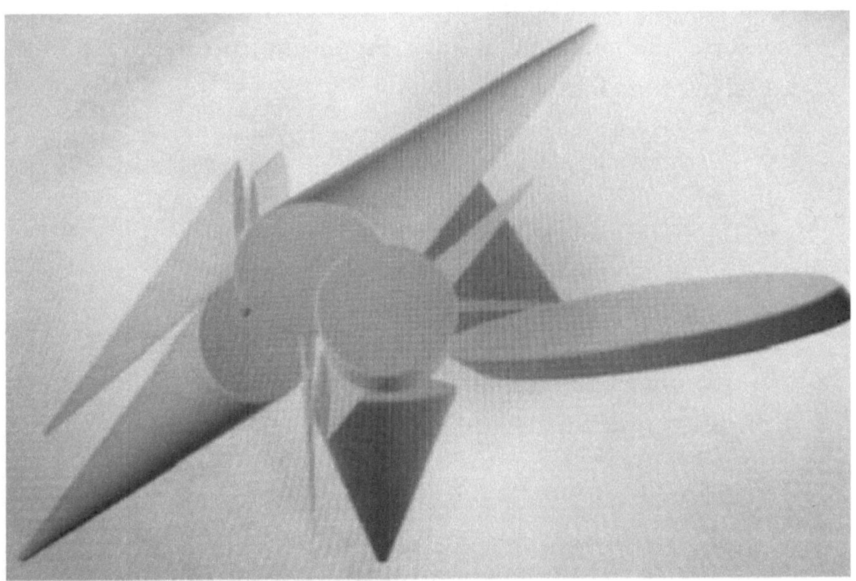

Gurdjieff taught that personality is legion.

It's what we pick up along the way.

We play host to a multiplicity of selves. There are scores of them, if not hundreds in each of us.

He said... few humans can cope with this concept, nor work within its implications.

Further, he states, humankind is irresponsibile to the godlike faculty of attention: he fails to mobilize it, he does not govern it. Our center moves from this identity to that. It hardens into self-pity, irritability, resentment, envy, vanity, hatred, every sort of negative emotion; it softens into treacherous interior fantasies, imagination, daydreams; it embellishes ignorance to masquerade as knowledge. The selves provide the power behind our inner and outer chattering and for the despotic associations which flitter ceaselessly through our weary brains.

It disguises the fact that a human is essentially an impersonal machine; an extraordinarily, complex, stimulus-response mechanism that eats impressions and excretes behavior. This human machine burns three fuel sources: food, air, and sensory impressions, fueling five centers, governing five functions:

* ❖ The intellectual center - thinking

* ❖ The emotional center - feeling

* ❖ The moving center - external movement

* ❖ The instinctive center - unlearned interior functions (digestive, respiratory, etc)

* ❖ The sex center - authentic sexual manifestations

While the design of this impersonal machine is exceptional... nothing really works properly. Unsupervised and uncalibrated, the centers relate inefficiently, jarring and grating each other. Some parts are overused, while some go unused.

While the situation is, perhaps, hopeless for the great mass of people, while imagining themselves free... for those who truly undertake the challenge through a frank and painful confrontation with this slavery of personalities and selves... Gurdjieff tells us... emancipation and the reentry of consciousness is possible.

He says... "Humankind is a unique machine on earth and can come to know itself as truly alive." Breathing proof of this can is dimly intuited, according to Gurdjieff, in such people as Christ, Pythagoras, Leonardo and perhaps some select moderns.

This hope of perfecting oneself is profoundly traditional in the Gurdjieff system of thought. Three religious ways have been opened to meet respective needs in small minorities of people in the past.

1. The Way of the fakir (subdues the body)
2. The Way of the monk (refines and dedicates feelings)
3. The Way of the yogi (cultivates intellectual powers)

Paradoxically, Gurdjieff goes by procedural not cultural labeling, thus a Bhakti yogi pursues "the way of the monk" and a Zen monk pursues "the way of the yogi".

These states of being lie within Gurdjieff's pantheon of development. Each of the three ways... leading to Man number four, demand exorbitant down payments, such as: behavioral constraints, celibacy, the wholesale renunciation of normal life... in return for development.

Gurdjieff does offer a shadowy tradition known as the "Fourth Way" or the "Way of the Sly Man." No dying to the world is required. It provides for the simultaneous and harmonious development of body, emotion, and intellect.

Humans of the Fourth Way accept normal circumstances, good or bad, money and sex all become indices of his being, parts of the field of struggle. Life is not just terrain crossed but becomes the guide itself

The historic lineage of this Way is obscure.

Societies of the past have been associated with the Fourth Way, according to Gurdjieff: Akhaldan, Heechtvori, Olbogmek, etc. These societies generally mean nothing to the history of religion or philosophy. Some say that the Fourth Way was present in the building of Mont St. Michel, the Cluniacs, the Templars, in Alchemists, early Quakers, the Russian Freemasons, and certain obscure schools of acting, music and craftsmanship.

The Fourth Way is suspected as being present wherever a special quality of attention and questioning was... or is, present.
Gurdjieff exacted no vows from his pupils. They wandered together through strange towns and unusual backwaters, learning sacred movement. He insisted they cultivate a critical mind, forbidding blind faith, replacing it with understanding. Through inner awareness, self-congratulation was replaced with an awed sense of being... under an entity, infinitely greater than oneself. Like the youthful Siddhartha, followers of Gurdjieff longed to penetrate their own nature and mystery.

What is being?
More exactly.... what is the quality of being-ness?
It is realizing a person's whole mass, their atomic weight, what he/she really can become.
It is not some bloated person belching out of hearsay learning, but rather a "learned individual." He says it is humankind's...."quotient of unity," it's gathered presence"... when truly Being, one begins to grasp what the Gurdjieff model of consciousness and the core of his teaching actually means.
Gurdjieff tells us... "We are asleep."
"Wake up!"

Franke Wednesday

The Lonely Woman

Cafes and nightclubs are a window on the world...
for those of us who spend our time in them.
From where I sit... on the stage
playing drums in a trio,
each night can be an indifferent drift,
or it can be a drama, depending on how you choose to view it.

To me, it's an endless parade of humanity.... each person with their own story, many of them sad, as it was with the Lonely Woman

Every once in a while she'd appear, sitting with a glass of wine on the periphery of the crowd, at a table, furthest away from everyone, on the far side of the terrace... overlooking the water. Always alone....

If she had sat in the middle, she would have drawn quite a bit of attention, because she was an attractive woman, with a kind of faraway look in her eye. But she kept to herself.

On breaks, I would go to the bar on the opposite side of the dance floor... and I'd sit in the last chair by the wall, order a Jack Daniels with a twist from Jake the bartender, and then I'd watch the world pass by. And though she didn't showup all that often, when she did, the tempo would pick up, and she'd have my full attention.

I often tasked myself, why didn't I just go over and introduce myself. But I expect it was because she wouldn't have wanted me to, me or anyone else, at least that's what I thought, and I respected her position. So, I decided to become an observer, rather than a participant.

Some people let you know what they feel without ever speaking. Just a glance tells you; it was that clear with her.

Then... one night she came in on the arm of a man. You could sense that she felt the missing piece had fallen into place... and the view was clearing. I watched them from the stage. They sat that night at her usual table on the terrace; they didn't talk much, just sat looking out at the ocean. Every once in awhile they'd lean towards each other, exchange a few words, smile, share a moment of private laughter, sit closer for a few minutes. Just before closing, as we were playing our last number, they got up and left... and after that I didn't see her for a long time.

And then... late one summer evening, she was back... sitting on the terrace... looking at the water, by herself. She left early that night.

Fall arrived, and with it, cooler winds.
And though I think of her often, I never saw the Lonely Woman again. I've often wondered... what was the story behind her, and if its life that makes some people unhappy and lonely, or if they're just born that way?

The nights are slower without her.

Audio script, Franke Wednesday

SID AND LUCKY TOGETHER

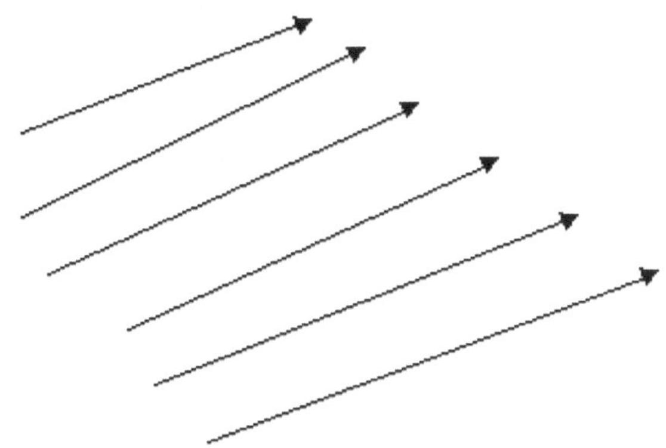

ON THE WAVEFRONT OF EXISTENCE

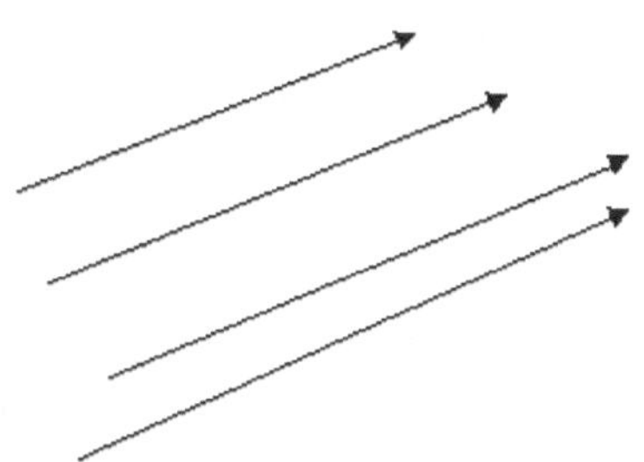

SID AND LUCKY research: the following information is drawn from...

<u>The Encyclopedia of the Akashic Record: Planet Earth</u>.

Search parameters

Sid and Lucky:

<u>see also</u>:

Poetic and sound artists

Inner self

Dharma bums

Spiritual seeking

Deviance

Ultimate truth

Lust and seeking

Artistic movements

Popular culture

Musical avant-garde

Post neurotic syndrome

Frequencies and evolution

Poetry of the soul

Abstracted by

William Morton Mertrain

Twenty First century Archivist/ Historian

His Comments

"There is thought electricity

that transforms those who express it... whether in art or music.

It permeates those who can sense or experience it.

It leaves a psychic imprint.

It is collaborative, not isolated in one solitary person or through solitary brilliance.

It is highly sought after by artistic explorers.

This fictional viewpoint that follows is excerpted from:
"A Sense of Vibration"
by P.D. Genovese and William Nowik
Copyright 2005
Virtual Putnam, NY, NY
Full Text Content: From: <u>The Sense of the Vibration</u>

The scene takes place in a real gone bar...
with a beat generation level of coolness.
There's high anticipation in the crowd... like that night in April 1960
when Coltrane left the Miles Davis group and began his first
performance with his own new group.
There was high expectation... a new edge was beginning,
a liminal vibration... they were speaking in poetic tongues."

Sid and Lucky's gig was set for the city of Prague...
at the Podzemí Klub... the Club Underground.
On opening night, the room was jammed...
with a line stretching outside.
The club was full of thieves and thinkers,
the desperate and the hopeful.
Energy was high, the place was "on fire."
It was a smoke-filled atmosphere, with talk a-buzzing."

The expectation was that something special was about to happen
and it was said to be
so good
and   so   strong...   that   it   would   defy   expectation.
____

Suddenly...

The houselights went dark
A single blue pin spot hit the stage from above.
Setting a mood ....

Then the first sounds,
a man encircled by musicians
at the back of the stage,
sheltered... in the blue hue of a second pin spot.
Low vibration and blue noise emanate... with distant feedback
explosions.
A poet sits on the corner of the stage.
She rises... and walks to the front of the stage, followed by a white pin
spot, and she says...
"Sid and Lucky.... Together on the Wavefront of Existence"
"Why did they come together...? after all those years...
and all the subtle, discordant differences of the past."
"Even before anything really happened
the mood on the street was expectant, based solely on rumor.
Things were about to get interesting."
"Everyone could feel it!"
"Damn!" the poet said. I feel it too."
"It's like... electric thought energy
It felt like... electrical thought energy.... surging through everyone's
imagination."
"It began as an inkling of what might happen, like a nervousness in the
pit of your stomach,
but it was there, it was real."

"People had heard that Sid was out of his shell
and Lucky was back from Afghanistan...
dragging his experimental sounds and spectacular gear."
"The talk was that they were getting together for one performance.

The street could sense it...
... electric thought energy."

"But very soon... it began dredging up all kinds of old memories.
It dredged up old memories in people. There was past history.
Not everyone was glad."

"But for the people who gauge the musical and artistic edge...
which had grown decidedly dull of late,
they knew it promised something,
and that something... was needed."
"Would things sharpen up?" that's what they wondered.

"From the very beginning
to the last step, Sid and Lucky had decided to
walk through the door of possibilities... together,
out into the open spaces beyond.
One question remained on everyone's mind ... why were they doing it?"

An African American sax player, standing with the musicians at the
back of the stage leaves the group and walks to the front of the stage...
He sits on a chair next to a small round table...the blue pin fades, and a
single white spot comes on above him. He lights a cigarette and says ...

"The Cause... What caused it to happen... is that what you want to
know?"
The Poet nods.
"Well... who can be sure? I think it was what Sid and Lucky found in
each other when they reconnected... something they just didn't find in
others... an openness... a daring."

"Don't get me wrong... they were both still carrying all the old bundles of time on their backs, filled with their past disputes. It's true, they had tried it all before."

"But after all the miles and experiences that they both had gone through... all the water under the bridge, the far-off places, the exotic relationships, Lucky's club in Korea, Sid's move to Beirut... all the forgotten and not so forgotten faces left behind... the disappointments...
Somehow, it still seemed worth it."

"They both wanted that ranting, raja of life that they had experienced before, and sometimes shared...
the mantras,
the trials
the tribulations
the beautiful and profound mistakes
the numerous dark nights of the soul... the women."

"Why did they come together you're asking?"
"Well... I think they found there was still something burning in them."
"Maybe it was inspiration, or a vision... perhaps just unrealized hopes...
Musicians are like that you know, we have secret aspirations, private visions that we dream of.
There had always been an undeniable connection between them, a tension true, but there was something similar that they both were after."
"They wanted the whole brewing, overflowing pot of it one more time!"
"And it was just there, waiting for the taking. I think that's how it was with Sid and Lucky."

He takes a drag off his cigarette. Waves a waitress over... orders a double scotch.
Once the drink arrives, he takes a deep slug and says...

"Now it's true that they were different in many ways, and that they often conflicted.
But along the inner seams, in their artistic core, there were common threads tying them together, and... maybe, it was because they were the last two left of the original mob ... of a certain breed in past history... the last two who still knew and cared why."

"But why?" said the poet walking towards him. "That's the question?"
The sax man looks up at the poet for a few moments... takes another sip of his scotch, then says, "Well... maybe they had a vision of what it could be... what was possible, you know".
"A belief in the creative act, uncorrupted."

"They remembered in the past, spontaneous moments they'd had spent together... in obscure halls and performance places, where they had worked together.
When something had jumped out of their selves and surprised them, enchanted them..."

"And though only a few people had been there to observe it ... Sid and Lucky remembered it had happened... and how... they both had been part of it... both had created it."
"Somehow, by using musical tools and cues...words, droning engines... feedback, or the sound of broken glass, it had manifested! And it could happen again."
"Whatever it was, it promised more to come."
"Yeah... maybe that's why... Sid and Lucky knew what was possible."

The sax man stands up... and continues talking to the poet...
"Now there are some people who reject Lucky... and Sid. They find fault
in them... in their style, or their musicianship, their attitude. But Sid
and Lucky knew, that down deep...

there was this promise... that they both wanted to meet."

Another voice shouts from off stage: "Things just never happened in
the past!"
The poet looks off stage... then she looks at the sax man, and says,
"Is that true? That's what their detractors say."
The voice off-stage (says doubtingly): "Sure there was promise; it was
always there... but it just didn't materialize." The sax man looks towards
the voice coming from off-stage and turns back to the poet.

"Yeah, I guess that's partly true, but I say.... let those who have eyes see
and those with ears, hear. And maybe there were reasons why it didn't
happen.
Like a boundary of quality that they both imposed on themselves..."
"Maybe it was their own sensitivity, or vulnerability...
maybe it was egotism... or the effects of the opinions of others."
"Maybe they weren't ready."
"Maybe they got distracted or aimed too high."
"Maybe they were sabotaged."
"Maybe! ... their frequencies were at odds."

The sax player turns to the audience... and speaks directly to them
"Both men had seen the world... been drawn to far off places, to the
exotic, to the dangerous."

"In their early meetings on Lucky's return, they shared their observations, secret insights, the thrill of distant people and lands they'd both traveled to. "

"They traded their stories, their private observations."

"They matched experiences, challenged each other... but respected that exploratory nature in each other. They recognized the survival tactics that each had used... shared dangers they had faced... the fear and the joy of it all."

"In their lives both men had rejected various things... repeatedly. Rejecting teachers,

rejecting Guru,

rejecting a firm commitment to a path."

"In some ways, Lucky had been more persistent... or perhaps, he'd succeeded or suffered from an inability to give up a certain identity he had of himself. He played the game well... to be the coolest cat... to have presence... to be a sage, an experimenter."

"Sid merged. Sid went within.

He withdrew into secret places, undertook esoteric pursuits, sought depth more than image."

Lucky flaunted... Sid disguised...

Lucky emanated... Sid searched."

The Poet interrupts... "But remember... the Cause... what was the cause? The big Why!"

The sax man turns to her, and says...

"Well... I've played with them both... they both have style; both can reside in or out of the pocket... you know what I mean?"

"Both are professionals, seasoned seekers, experienced travelers."

"These are their connectors... also, a certain musical confidence in themselves and in each other. More importantly, Sid and Lucky believe in the spontaneous as a springboard to create unanticipated opportunities. It is what stylized their reputations, scared some away... they were masters of the spontaneous."

"Now it's true that both elicited some serious reactions in people... some people loved them,
while others lacked that appreciation. In fact, they rejected them. It was almost unavoidable...
their sounds were just too far out for some."
"On the other hand, at times negative reactions were instigated, initiated by Sid or Lucky themselves... their rebuttal and disdain for the doubters and detractors."

Yet the poet persisted...
"But the cause...What was the cause?"
The saxman was getting annoyed...
"Listen I've been telling you...can't you hear? I thought you were a poet?"
"When the spontaneous... met opportunity,
it put Sid and Lucky
in the same place
at the same time,
together
and with so much promise... it merged with a sense that time, if it wasn't running out...
it was at least becoming more limited.
And they both wanted it!
A cause was a common desire, a belief; the need to make it happen!"

"And so, it is happening..." says the Sax man, spreading his arms wide
and circling them.
The lights on the stage go black...
An upright bass line begins... a funky, bluesy line, as the sax man picks
up his horn and begins a groove over the top. A blue spotlight is on
above him; when he stops playing, he begins speaking again...

"While traveling on the Silk Road of life,
human beings pass each other,
some are ignored and stay apart
others draw together,
and are remembered... valued,
they leave an impression.
They touch those that they encounter."

"Some people... we hope more from... but don't get it.
Others we promise something to... but can't deliver.
Disappointments and regrets are scattered all along the road of life...
Sid and Lucky remembered each other... in many of those ways."

"Yet they found something
inhabiting each other, that they didn't find in elsewhere
something special,
something to believe in...
to hope for,
to a take a last chance on."
"Along the dry deserts and lonely valleys
that the long road of life winds through
people tire
people stop
are diverted
become daunted."

"Most survivors have forgotten their... original prime objective.
They get mixed up
corrupted,
standardized,
or normalized,
sometimes even fictionalized.
They mobilize... solely for the art of survival,
for seeking the best advantage."
"They're even become convinced ....
it's sophisticated to think that way."
"They think it's mature to forget their prime objective. The original
dream...
That it makes them more successful, smarter to change... or rearrange...
to become realistic!"

"But Sid and Lucky... they remembered the original purpose.
the thrill of the creative act, the big bang in it!"
"That's what locked them together, if only momentarily."
"Sound and frequencies... words as triggers...
everything as a catalyst for inspired moments.
These things glued them together!"

"Now perhaps Sid and Lucky
imagined things about themselves... about each other,
that weren't necessarily completely true."
"Possibly, they allowed this to infect their thinking...
But they were survivors, explorers and in full do-mode.
And to succeed, each had something that the other needed."

"What brought them together... you ask?"
"It was the need for an outcome...
The cause was the pursuit of an outcome!"

They were committed... to express their inner intent,
to silence the doubters, to see what came out
to take the time
to create their own form of spontaneous truth."
The Saxman says...
"So, at this moment,
in this specific stretch of time,
Sid and Lucky are together again,
abandoning nothingness and solitary striving."

"They're riding on the wavefront of existence
forsaking hopelessness...
together, in the same place,
creating...
perhaps for the last time.
It is their moment; their time."

"Sid and Lucky... Together on the Wavefront of Existence."

The Lights dim... Applause rises from the crowd...
Two spots following Sid and Lucky as they walk out from each side of
the stage... and so the performance begins.
End Full Text Content: From: <u>The Sense of the Vibration</u>
Franke Wednesday/ Rochester, New York
October 26, 2001

Life is a tricky thing

Franke Wednesday

It sneaks up on you
And suddenly, years have gone by
You thought you were enlightened
seeking the higher plane,
only to find that you were
not... enlightened,
but rather painfully human, an imperfect being.

Friends, once so dear,
are no longer near... they have become disconnected.
Why do these things happen?
Sometimes quickly... other times, silently.
We are all too self-absorbed
too caught up in the moment
too unto our own selves and purposes...
to notice

We ply our trades, exposing questionable tirades,
ever caught up in the drama of life.
Yet all around us
sacred acts are occurring...
so near... yet, we are too blind to see.
Turnabout
Stanza Two
O`Koo Bakata
Moreu

While all around us
sacred acts are occurring
so near... yet so far away.

135

Lost Essence

I was lost in a place without direction
Amidst a barrage of hodgepodge.
Having missed the path years ago,
I now, desperately, saw the situation...
felt a kind of realization.
No longer young or even middle-aged,
yet the goal remained elusive.
The condition was becoming dire...
How to overcome this wave of doubt and disillusionment?
What could bring revelation?
Foreign lands, foreign thoughts?
What could bring transformation?

In the past, in those days gone by,
I saw it... right up ahead!
Granted, it was through a gossamer curtain... but it was imminent.
The search was energetic, confidant
accumulating essences... eternal bits of the puzzle... swirled all around
me.

There had been highlights,
High moments
Years of elated striving
clear goals & possibilities.
Indeed... flashes of brilliance.
But now... where had it gone?

Instead....I hover on the periphery
moving towards the frontier,

ever closer to the borderland
traveling the road of diminishing mortality.

So, I speak in a dialect of the inner self,
private conversations within...
filled with remaining questions, like...
What will we leave behind in those we've touched?
In those we have had some part in shaping.
What will remain after we are gone?
Fleeting memories for a generation...
What will be left of us after we are gone?
Tiny Bits of expressions, traces... somehow still alive within those we
have affected?
Recollections lingering for a decade or two... a few stories housed in the
annals of family history?

Or could it go deeper... a genetic anomaly... pieces of our character
leaving an anonymous imprint... a creative mutation within our
descendants... appearing someday in a new self... with a new future?
What is still left to be imparted.... and to whom?
What must be completed in our... human mission?

Through all these questions... I persist, waiting,
praying for a final chance to align my soul
with the Great Mystery
To make it so...

I was lost in a place without direction
Amidst a barrage of hodgepodge
Adrift... without direction
in a puddle of lost essence.
Franke Wednesday

Night after Night

Franz would sit at his desk in the evening and wait for something to materialize, to rise up, like a specter from the complex agar-agar of his mind. He had expected something tangible for a long time; a consolidation of one of the dozens of creations that he had logged in the file cabinet of his brain over the decades. He had expected these thoughts, these embodiments of his interior life would manifest into a culmination of his artistic and intellectual curiosity.

Yet... night after night... only scraps emerged from short bursts of clarity.
No grand story surfaced... nor the dedication required to find it. Tableaus of past storylines would arise, a product of the obsessive shifting research he had pursued through years of intense effort, boring deeply into regions, divining subtleties of obscure cultures, reaching an apogee of focus during various productive eras and epochs of his life.

But lately, he had sensed a turning away, a rejecting of these creations he had strived towards. He found it all very strange. Perhaps, he thought, he had already given these ideas lives of their own, within his inner life, an existence that no one would ever know about... but still residing in the subliminal recesses of his mind.

"Perhaps this process has served some purpose, a formula needed in natural selection."

It left him feeling a great sadness; he held his visions in such affection. They were a part of his being. The anxiety he experienced trying to bring his inner thoughts into fruition, seemed to him part of an ancient, very personal purpose... one that he now thought he was unlikely to achieve, and perhaps, was no longer necessary... and possibly was becoming an impediment to future growth, stalling him from moving towards a new, still undetermined purpose.

It started when he began experiencing a series of semi-focused moments, visions and waking dreams that temporarily occupied his mind... when he slept, his sleeping dreams also contained visions... or visions would materialize in the form of drifting daydreams.

Images and sounds would float through his mind... an etheric reverie, gently pushed by kaleidoscopic moving mirages, wafting towards him, capturing his awareness, absorbing him, & then... passing through his consciousness out to obscurity.

He longed to fully understand what they were, why they were happening, what they represented; to learn where they were coming from, and how he could immerse himself more completely in them.

Something essential seemed to be happening, at times both compelling and confusing, then, just as quickly, they would become elusive and disappear.

He waited for the visions to emerge with intense interest. Then, when they did... strange people in some ancient time, vaguely familiar would appear... they seemed to be moving through a world fresher and more dangerous than his own. Complete scenes would sometime occur, riveting his attention, and then, disappearing just as suddenly, leaving him longing for a return to the vision.

As the days passed, he left his room less and less often. He began to feel himself slipping into a kind of fog, one that never really cleared.

It was like looking at something from the corner of your eye, an old Sufi technique, and unexpectedly, seeing a luminous spirit for an instant, leaving you wondering whether what you saw was real... and needing to see it again!

He began to worry that he might be slipping into some sort of delusional state, perhaps even... a form of madness.

Franke Wednesday

Love is alive

She taught me true love.
Not just for a man and a woman, but the very soul of the heart, the pure blazing center. Light manifests around her...
in her children, in people she barely knows,
something that endears her to them. like a secret that they can't quite explain. It deepens each day into a silent sob and is almost too much to contain... this beautiful sense of love.
Why does it take us so long to learn... to see? How unbearable is the thought of separation? or.... in the now foreseeable future,
life without one... or the other
Like leaves falling from a brilliant maple tree, they depart, eventually dropping one at a time... unto the moist soil. For each leaf that falls a dear has left... and now are waiting ahead. To them... we send this message... Love is alive on Earth!
Franke Wednesday

Looking for Pearls....

Audio script, Franke Wednesday

He'd taken a slow boat from Jondapour to the mainland, and he could see the lights of a port along the coast as the ship drew closer to the harbor.

Somewhere on the Arufura Sea... in 1923

It was late-night when the ship finally moored in the drowsy port town. A kind of silent haze was hanging over the docks. As he came down the gangplank, he could hear music coming from some honkytonk in the distance. He needed to find a place to stay.

He noticed the buildings of the town were quite old and the street was made of fitted stone, probably both remnants of early Portuguese times. Two people skirted through a gloomy side street, keeping to themselves, then disappearing around a corner

Darkness had fallen and most of the town was asleep.

He stopped for a moment to look behind him, where the waxing moon was reflecting off the water of the harbor... illuminating the tramp steamers docked there, including the one he had come in on... the Sarawak Star.

Why he had left Jondapour was troubling him. There was a pattern emerging. Just when he was comfortable, and he should stay in a place... he would leave. He couldn't seem to settle. It was baffling to him. His restlessness had led him from one obscure port to another.

"Hmmm...." he took a deep breath in and thought, "the air is sweet tonight." He could taste the sea air and the salt, and there was the smell of fish and he noticed some purple bougainvillea growing on the wall of a building. The fragrance of sweet flowers wafted in on the wind.

As he gazed above the buildings, beyond the town, he could see in the distance a low range of hills... and further out, the moonlight and stars silhouetted larger mountains in the interior... rather dim and foreboding.
He pulled his trilby down low on his forehead, picked up his suitcase and began walking away from the ship towards the town.

He had heard from a sailor on board the Sarawak Star, about a road that ran along the coast. The man had said, "if you head west, the road will wind along the shoreline, through small, coastal villages with the ocean crashing in, and then... you'll pass through a great mangrove swamp. Finally, after some miles further on, at the far end of the island, the road will lead you down to a beautiful cove with white sand beaches. "And there," he said, "you'll find smaller, simpler villages, where the people still follow the old ways.... the old beliefs."

"And every morning, the brave boys of the village free dive deep onto the ocean floor, where they search for oysters... with pearls in them... and the nights are quiet... and the girls are sweet."

He had been looking for something, something that he just couldn't seem to find. It was mystical. He felt this emptiness inside from not knowing or remembering who he was. It was a fight against the emptiness. He kept moving because, he thought...maybe, somewhere, in some odd corner of the world, there would be...
a revelation

a wise man
he'd have a vision
find a drug
something …. that would provide answers.

That's what he believed anyway... way down deep inside. And, as he walked toward the town, he began feeling a kind of hope.

"Maybe," he thought, "he would take that ride along the coast.
He'd look for those white beaches... and see what was hidden in the coves....
And maybe he'd find a pearl... just maybe... a pearl of different kind"

***

At some point in the future, another freighter is crossing the inner sea, following along the islands of the great archipelago. Steam would be pouring out of its' single stack and trailing for miles behind the ship. Dark, ominous clouds would be hanging low in the sky.
On board, the captain would urge his men... "Secure the cargo there! Tie it down, there's a storm a brewing!!!"

And... on the bow of the ship, a solitary passenger would be standing, staring out towards the horizon, his coat pulled tightly around his neck and a cold wind pushing hard against him.

He's looking for something... something he hopes to find. Maybe, he'll uncover it in the next port, or the next...

Still looking for pearls....

Don't miss out!

Visit the website below and you can sign up to receive emails whenever Peter Genovese publishes a new book. There's no charge and no obligation.

https://books2read.com/r/B-A-LMON-MUGXB

BOOKS 2 READ

Connecting independent readers to independent writers.

Also by Peter Genovese

Lost utk'Irtana
Immortal Memories In Lost utk'Irtana

Standalone
Karmic Debris: The Poetic Writings of Franke Wednesday and Piya
Italia

About the Author

Peter Genovese is a writer, musician, global consultant, off the path traveler, academic, and Librarian. He has created Karmic Debris so that the words contained within would not be lost, nor those years of striving and growth be forgotten.

His novel is entitled _Immortal Memories In Lost utk'Irtana_